Contents

About this book   1
Electrical parts   2
Safety warnings   2
Coloured spinning disc ①   3
Hand held fan ①   6
Torch ①   8
Wire loop game ①   12
Fan boat ①   15
Brush monster ②   18
Electric buggy ②   21
Paddle boat ②   26
Cereal racer ②   30
Chair-o-plane ②   34
Lighthouse ③   38
Motorbike③   43
Autorickshaw ③   48
Paper dart launcher ③   54

Difficulty Level: Easier ①   Medium ②   Harder ③

About this book

This book introduces children to basic electrical circuits, then brings the circuits to life by using them to make working models. It helps children understand how things work, for example if you make a bulb circuit and mount it in an old drinks bottle it becomes a torch. The book also helps children learn how to fix things when they go wrong.

All the projects in this book can be made with a single kit of electrical parts. Once you have finished with one model you can dismantle it to make another, and then another. Possible suppliers and part numbers are listed on the website www.technologyforfun.co.uk.

Many of the projects use low temperature melt glue guns or double sided foam sticky tape to join things together, available from DIY shops, craft shops or the internet. If using foam sticky tape then 12 mm wide, 1 to 1.5 mm thick with strong adhesive is recommended.

Look out for this picture of Einstein to find an explanation of the science behind the projects.

Electrical Parts (see www.technologyforfun.co.uk for where to buy)

Battery holder with two AA batteries fitted

Motor with robust connectors

Motor mount

3V bulb in bulb holder

Battery clip

Crocodile leads

Propeller

Toggle (on/off) switch with thread and nut

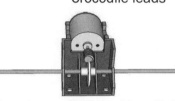
Motor/worm gearbox with ~ 40:1 speed reduction (clip-in version)

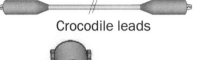
Motor/worm gearbox ~ 40:1 speed reducti (screw mounted vers)

⚠ Safety warnings

1. Look out for this warning triangle to spot safety warnings in the text.

2. If using a glue gun be careful not to burn yourself, as the glue can be very hot. Make sure you use a low temperature melt glue gun.

3. Always ask a responsible adult to use the Stanley knife on your behalf. Younger readers will also need a responsible adult to assist them when using secateurs, saws and electric drills.

4. If your batteries are 'short-circuited' they will get very hot. To avoid this do not connect the wires from the battery terminals directly together; they must be connected across the motor or lamp. Also:

i. When not using the batteries it is advisable to remove the battery clip from the battery holder.

ii. Tie the black wire from the battery clip around the red wire as shown below. This makes the wires different lengths, so the bare ends are less likely to touch.

iii. Make sure the insulated sleeves cover the crocodile clips to prevent short-circuits if the clips touch.

Coloured spinning disc

You will need:

- Battery holder with two AA batteries fitted
- Battery clip
- Toggle switch
- Motor and motor mount
- 3 crocodile leads
- 2 small rubber bands (2 cm to 5 cm long)
- White card
- Empty biro ink tube which slides onto the motor shaft (e.g. Bic - some are too narrow)
- Pair of compasses
- Scissors
- Coloured felt tip pens

1. Make the following circuit:

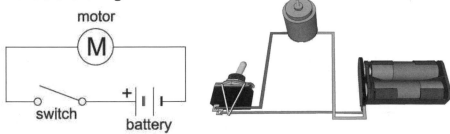

i.   Attach the battery clip firmly to the battery holder.

ii. Take a crocodile lead and clip one end to the red wire from the battery clip. Clip the other end to one of the terminals on the toggle switch.

iii. Take a second crocodile lead and clip one end onto one of the terminals on the motor and the other end onto the free switch terminal.

iv. Stretch one of the small rubber bands over the switch body and crocodile clips as shown. This should prevent the crocodile clips falling off.

v.   Take the third crocodile lead and clip one end to the black wire from the battery clip and the other end to the free terminal on the motor.

vi. Make sure the insulated sleeves are covering the crocodile clip jaws to prevent them touching each other and causing a short circuit.

vii. Switch on and check the motor shaft goes round. Switch off and check that it stops.

viii. If the motor shaft goes round, fold the crocodile leads neatly and hold them together with the second rubber band. This is to stop the crocodile leads coming off the wires from the battery clip.

ix. If the motor shaft doesn't go round then check your connections are not loose. Make sure the crocodile clips are connected onto the bare wires themselves, not onto the coloured insulation on the wires.

x.   If the motor shaft still doesn't go round remove the battery clip and crocodile clips. Press the motor terminals directly against the battery terminals. If the motor shaft doesn't turn you probably have a flat battery, or possibly a damaged motor. If it does turn then re-introduce the leads one by one.

2.   Using the pair of compasses, draw a 50 mm diameter circle in the white card. Cut it out with the scissors and colour in using felt tip pens. You can try whichever colours and designs you like. Some examples are shown below.

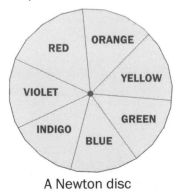

A Newton disc

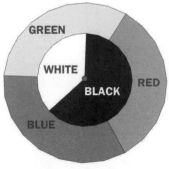

Maxwell's disc

Benham's disc

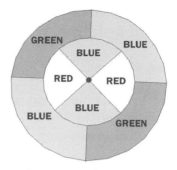

Primary colours

3. Slide the disc onto the motor shaft as shown on the right, using the hole made by the compasses.

4. Cut a 5 mm length off the open end of the biro ink tube using the scissors. Slide it over the motor shaft to hold the disc in place.

5. Either hold the motor with the disc facing up or clip it into the motor mount and rest it on a table. Switch on and see the effects you get.

A Newton disc has a segment from each colour of the rainbow. When you spin it, you should see the colours combine to white (or nearly white). A rainbow is caused by white light from the sun being split up into its component colours by water drops, so if you mix all the rainbow colours you would expect to get white light. This is not the same as mixing paints; mixing paints of all the colours of the rainbow gives brown.

Maxwell got a similar effect by mixing just red, green and blue and trying to match this with the white/black mix in the centre of the disc.

When you spin Benham's black and white disc you should see arcs of pale colour; this is an optical illusion caused by the colour vision cells in your eyes responding at different rates to the white flash. Not everyone sees the same colours.

The final disc is just an example of mixing primary colours. Mixing blue and green light should give cyan (similar to turquoise), whilst mixing blue and red should give magenta (a kind of purple).

Hand held fan

You will need:

- Battery holder with two AA batteries fitted
- Battery clip
- Toggle switch
- Motor
- Propeller
- 3 crocodile leads
- 2 small rubber bands (2 cm to 5 cm long)
- Clean dry plastic drinks bottle e.g. the larger size Fruit Shoot bottle, Lucozade or Lucozade Sport – the neck must be big enough to fit the motor in. If you use a transparent bottle with the label removed you can show people how the fan works.
- Transparent sticky tape e.g. Sellotape
- Double sided foam sticky tape
- Sharp nail scissors

1. Make the following circuit and check that it works. See section 1 of the coloured spinning disc project on pages 3-4 for more details of how to do this.

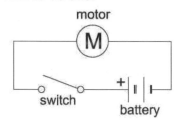
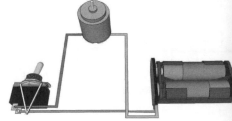

2. Press the propeller onto the motor shaft. Hold the motor with the propeller facing upwards, switch on and check the propeller goes round.

 Do not hold the propeller near your eyes. Do not put your finger in the way of the propeller when it is turning as it hurts.

3. Check that the propeller is blowing the air away from the motor. If not then swap over the crocodile clips attached to the motor terminals. Make sure it is now blowing air the other way.

4. Switch off and check the propeller stops. Remove the propeller.

5. Remove the lid and cut the drinks bottle as follows:

i) Use the sharp nail scissors to pierce the bottle just above where it narrows at the waist. Cut all the way round.

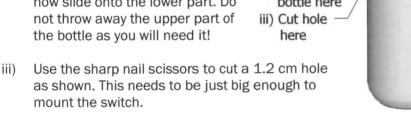

ii) Trim an additional 5 mm off the upper part of the bottle as shown. The upper part of the bottle should now slide onto the lower part. Do not throw away the upper part of the bottle as you will need it!

i) Cut around bottle here
ii) Cut around bottle here
iii) Cut hole here

iii) Use the sharp nail scissors to cut a 1.2 cm hole as shown. This needs to be just big enough to mount the switch.

6. Place the battery holder and clip, with crocodile leads attached, in the bottom of the bottle.

7. Unscrew the nut from the switch and remove the on/off label (if fitted). Push the threaded part of the switch through the hole from the inside, then replace the on/off label and screw the nut on firmly as shown.

label
nut

8. Wind a layer of foam sticky tape around the motor. Remove the plastic backing from the foam tape and push the motor up into the neck of the bottle so that the whole of the motor shaft is sticking out. You may need more than one layer of foam tape, depending on the size of the bottle neck.

motor

9. Push the crocodile leads into the bottle, being careful not to cause a short circuit by touching bare metal parts together. Slide the upper part of the bottle onto the lower part and secure with Sellotape.

10. Fit the propeller back onto the motor shaft. Make sure it is not touching the bottle neck.

11. Try out your fan, being careful not to put the propeller near your eyes. If you have long hair try not to get it tangled up in the propeller!

The fan works by producing a stream of air as the propeller turns. The blades are set at an angle; this means that when the propeller turns it pushes the air upwards as shown below. You may notice that the propeller is curved to help scoop up the air – this means it will work better in one direction than the other.

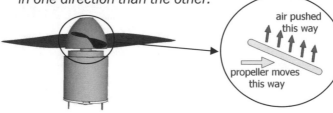

air pushed this way

propeller moves this way

Torch

Easier ①

You will need:

- Battery holder with two AA batteries fitted
- Battery clip
- Toggle switch
- Lamp holder with 3V bulb fitted
- 3 crocodile leads
- 2 small rubber bands (2 cm to 5 cm long)
- Clean dry plastic drinks bottle e.g. the larger Fruit Shoot bottle. You need one which is quite wide just below the neck, so that the bulb can be pushed well into the neck of the bottle
- Coca Cola, Diet Coke or Coke Zero aluminium drinks can
- Transparent plastic e.g. display panel from a cake or biscuit box
- Transparent sticky tape e.g. Sellotape
- Double sided foam sticky tape
- Scissors and sharp nail scissors
- Ruler and felt tip pen
- Responsible adult with a Stanley knife

1. Make the following circuit:

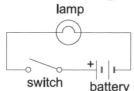

i) Attach the battery clip firmly to the battery holder.

ii) Take a crocodile lead and clip one end to the red wire from the battery clip. Clip the other end to one of the terminals on the toggle switch.

iii) Take a second crocodile lead and clip one end onto one of the terminals on the underside of the lamp holder and the other end to the free switch terminal.

iv) Stretch one of the small rubber bands over the switch body and crocodile clips as shown. This should prevent the crocodile clips falling off.

v) Take the third crocodile lead and clip one end to the black wire from the battery clip and the other end to the free terminal on the underside of the lamp holder.

vi) On some lamp holders the screw doesn't stick out far enough to clip onto. Fit a longer screw if you have one. Otherwise unscrew using a screwdriver and clamp the bare metal end of the black wire from the battery clip under the head of the screw.

vii) Make sure the insulated sleeves are covering the crocodile clip jaws to prevent them touching each other and causing a short circuit.

viii) Switch on and check the bulb lights up. Switch off and check it goes out. If the bulb doesn't light up then check your connections are not loose. Make sure the crocodile clips are connected to the wires themselves, not onto the coloured insulation.

ix) If the bulb still doesn't light up, remove the battery clip and crocodile clips. Press the battery terminals directly against the screws on the back of the bulb holder. If the bulb doesn't light you could have a flat battery, or possibly a damaged bulb. If it does then re-introduce the leads one at a time.

2.   Remove the lid and cut the drinks bottle as follows:

i)   Use the sharp nail scissors to pierce the bottle where it narrows at the waist, then cut all the way round.

ii)   Trim an additional 5 mm off the upper part of the bottle as shown. The upper part of the bottle should now slide onto the lower part. Do not throw away the upper part of the bottle as you will need it!

i) Cut around bottle here

ii) Cut around bottle here

iii) Cut hole here

iii)   Use the sharp nail scissors to cut a 1.2 cm hole as shown. This needs to be just big enough to mount the switch.

3.   Ask a responsible adult to cut the top and bottom 2 cm off the aluminium drinks can using the Stanley knife. Throw away the ends – these can be sharp.

 It is very important not to use a steel can, e.g. a baked bean can. These can be extremely sharp.

2.5 cm

cylinder of aluminium

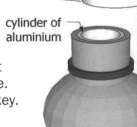

4.   Slit the can along its length using the scissors and flatten it out. Using the ruler and felt tip pen, mark out a rectangle 2.5 cm x 7.8 cm on the can. Cut it out using the scissors and roll it into a cylinder with the shiny side on the inside. Throw away any trimmings as they can be spikey.

5.   Slide the cylinder into the neck of the bottle. It will act as a reflector.

strips of double sided foam sticky tape

6.   Cut two squares of foam sticky tape and stick them onto the tops of the two lamp holder terminals. The terminals must not touch the aluminium cylinder; this would cause a short circuit.

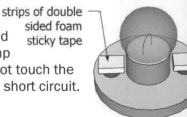

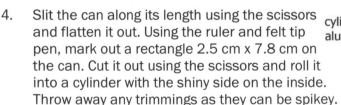

7. Remove the plastic backing from the foam tape and stick the bulb holder into the upper part of the bottle so that the bulb is located in the neck of the bottle.

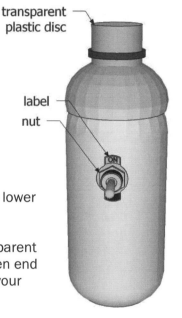
bulb

8. Unscrew the nut from the switch and remove the metal on/off label (if fitted). Push the threaded part of the switch through the hole from the inside, then replace the on-off label and screw the nut on firmly.

transparent plastic disc

9. Put the battery holder and clip, with crocodile leads attached, in the bottom of the bottle with the battery clip uppermost.

label

nut

10. When pushing the crocodile leads into the bottle, be careful not to create a short circuit by touching bare metal parts together.

11. Slide the upper part of the bottle onto the lower part as shown and secure with Sellotape.

12. Cut a 3 cm diameter disc out of the transparent plastic sheet and Sellotape it over the open end of your bottle, then switch on and try out your torch.

When you switch on the torch chemical energy stored in the batteries is converted into electrical energy. The bulb has a very thin wire (filament) made of a metal with a high melting point such as tungsten.

When the electricity passes through the filament it gets very hot and glows brightly, giving off light and heat energy. Sometimes the filament can get too hot and melt –we say that the bulb has 'blown'.

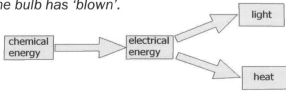

chemical energy → electrical energy → light / heat

Wire loop game

You will need:

- Battery holder with two AA batteries fitted
- Battery clip
- Toggle switch
- Lamp holder with 3V bulb fitted
- 4 crocodile leads
- Small rubber band (2 cm to 5 cm long)
- Wood, hardboard or plastic board approximately
  3 mm thick x 25 cm x 25 cm
- Wine cork
- Bare aluminium wire approximately 2 mm to 3 mm in diameter
  (alternatively you could use a bare wire coat hanger)
- Wire cutters and pliers
- Hand drill and 5 mm drill bit
- Vice or G-clamp and spare piece of wood
- Glue gun or sticky tape

1. Make the following circuit and check that it works. Clip the crocodile leads onto the screw heads on top of the lamp holder, not to the underside. Other than that, see section 1 of the torch project on pages 9-10 for more details of how to do this.

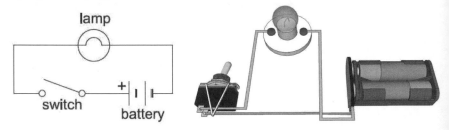

2. Cut a piece of wire about 1 metre long using the wire cutters. (You may need to bend the wire backwards and forwards a few times to break it off.)

3. Clamp the board in the vice or onto the spare piece of wood so that you don't drill into your table. Drill four holes in the board, in roughly the positions shown. It is better if they are not in a straight line.

4. Poke one end of the wire down though hole 1. Bend it sharply and poke it back up through hole 2; you may need to use the pliers. Make the wire lie flat along the bottom surface. Bend the end flat along the top surface.

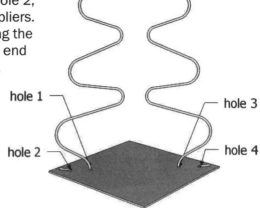

wire shape

hole 1

hole 2

hole 3

hole 4

5. Bend the remainder of the wire into a shape of your choice. It needs to be quite difficult to follow but not impossible.

6. Push the other end of the wire down through hole 3 and back up through hole 4. Make it lie flat along the bottom surface. (You can cover the wire on the bottom surface with sticky tape to help stop it scratching the table.) Bend the end flat along the top surface.

7. Clamp the cork in the vice and drill a hole through the middle as shown on the right.

8. Cut a length of wire about 15 cm long. Use the pliers to loop it around your wire shape and push the end through the cork as shown below. Attach the bulb holder, battery holder and switch to the board as shown using a glue gun or sticky tape. If using a glue gun just use a dab of glue; then it will be easy to take the components off when you want to reuse them for your next project.

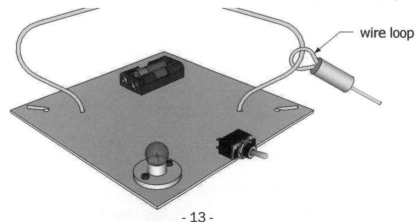

wire loop

9. Unclip one of the crocodile clips from the lamp. Clip it onto the end of the wire shape as shown below. Use the fourth crocodile lead to connect the bare end of the loop to the free terminal on the lamp.

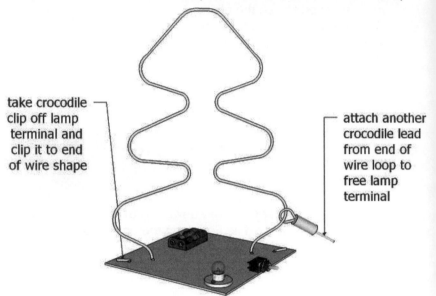

take crocodile clip off lamp terminal and clip it to end of wire shape

attach another crocodile lead from end of wire loop to free lamp terminal

10. Switch on and try out your wire loop game. The aim is to try and move the loop all the way round the wire shape without touching it. If you touch it the lamp should come on. If it is too easy you can reduce the size of the loop or adjust the wire shape to make it more complicated. If it is too difficult you can make the loop bigger.

The combination of the wire shape and the wire loop acts like a switch. They are both are made of metal and are good conductors of electricity. When the loop touches the wire shape the circuit is completed and the lamp comes on. If you have a 3V buzzer (as shown below left) you could connect this as well as the lamp (as shown below right), or instead of it. These buzzers only work one way round, so if it doesn't work then swap the buzzer connections over.

buzzer (optional)

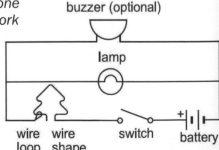

lamp

buzzer

wire loop   wire shape   switch   battery

Fan powered boat

Easier ①

You will need:

- Battery holder with two AA batteries fitted
- Battery clip
- Toggle switch
- Motor and motor mount
- Propeller
- 3 crocodile leads
- 2 small rubber bands (2 cm to 5 cm long)
- 2 small plastic bags e.g. sandwich bags or smaller
- Plastic pot with straight sides about 7 cm tall by 3.5 cm in diameter
- 3 large polystyrene foam pizza bases
- Felt tip pen and ruler
- Large pair of sharp scissors or responsible adult with a Stanley knife
- Glue gun or double sided foam tape
- Sticky tape e.g. Sellotape

1. Use the felt tip pen and ruler to mark out a boat shape on one of the pizza bases. Make it quite wide (at least 14 cm) and use the whole length of the pizza base as shown.

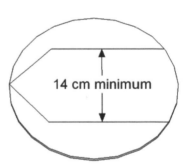

2. Cut out using the sharp scissors, or ask a responsible adult with a Stanley knife to cut it out for you.

3. Use this boat shape as a template to draw another one on the second pizza base, and cut this one out as well.

4. Stick the two boat shapes together using glue or foam tape all the way round.

5. Stick the plastic pot towards the rear of the boat as shown on the following page using glue or foam tape.

6. Use the felt tip pen and ruler to mark out a rectangle about 8 cm wide by 10 cm long on the third pizza base. Cut it out, use it as a template to make another one and stick them together. Stick them towards the front of the boat. This is to make a raised platform to help prevent the batteries getting wet.

7. Make the following circuit and check that it works. See section 1 of the coloured spinning disc project on pages 3-4 for more details of how to do this.

8. Press the propeller onto the motor shaft. Clip the motor into the motor mount and stick to the top of the pot. You can try the propeller facing backwards or forwards; it may work better one way than the other. It must not touch the pot or the pizza base when it turns. You may need to slide the motor so that it protrudes (sticks out) from its mount to achieve this.

leave gap between propeller and pot

9. Switch on and check the propeller goes round.

 Do not hold the propeller near your eyes. Do not put your finger in the way of the propeller when it is turning, as it hurts.

10. Check that the propeller is blowing the air towards the back of the boat. If not then swap over the two crocodile clips on the back of the motor. Make sure it is now blowing air towards the back of the boat. Switch off again.

11. Put the battery holder and the switch into the two small plastic bags with the wires sticking out. Seal them with sticky tape to prevent water getting in.

12. Place the batteries towards the front of the boat on the raised platform. Balance the boat on the side of your hand as shown and check that the centre of gravity is roughly in the middle. You can move the batteries forwards or backwards to achieve this.

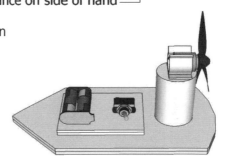

balance on side of hand ⟶

13. Position the switch in between the battery holder and the plastic pot as shown here. Tape the battery holder and switch in their plastic bags onto the raised platform.

14. Switch on and make sure the propeller still goes round. If it doesn't then it may be catching on the plastic pot, or one of the connections may have come loose.

15. Try out the boat in a bath, water tray, paddling pool or similar. You may wish to make some alterations, e.g. by adding sides and a 'wheel house'. If the boat turns to one side you could add a keel or fins along the sides to help it go straight.

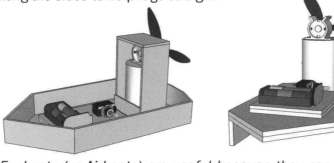

Fanboats (or Airboats) are useful because they can operate in very shallow water. The propeller is housed in a metal cage to stop it from injuring people. Fanboats are commonly used for transport in the Florida Everglades, USA. When Hurricane Katrina hit New Orleans causing widespread flooding, fan boats were used to rescue thousands of people. They can also be used on ice to rescue people from frozen lakes.

Brush monster

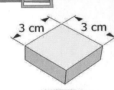

Medium ②

You will need:

- Battery holder with two AA batteries fitted
- Battery clip
- Toggle switch
- Motor and motor mount
- 3 crocodile leads
- Small rubber band (2 cm to 5 cm long)
- Hand brush (as in dustpan and brush) – you need one with sloping bristles. It should be quite wide so that it doesn't fall over.
- 1 to 1.2 cm thick wood offcut (at least 3 cm wide by 8 cm long)
- Wooden wheel 3.8 cm diameter x 1.2 cm thick (optional)
- Pair of compasses (if not using a wooden wheel)
- 7 large cable ties (~ 20 cm long)
- Pencil and ruler
- Wood saw and wood file
- G-clamp or vice
- Hand drill and 2 mm drill bit
- Scissors
- Decorations, e.g. plastic eyes, pipe cleaners, feathers
- Glue gun or double sided foam tape

cable tie

1. Make the following circuit and check that it works. See section 1 of the coloured spinning disc project on pages 3-4 for more details of how to do this.

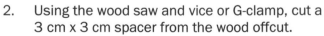

motor

switch

battery

2. Using the wood saw and vice or G-clamp, cut a 3 cm x 3 cm spacer from the wood offcut.

3. If not using a ready made wheel, draw a 4 cm diameter circle on the remaining wood using the pair of compasses. Cut it roughly to size using the saw and round off using the file.

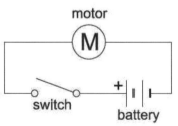

3 cm   3 cm

4 cm diameter

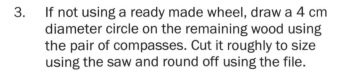

4. Drill a 2 mm diameter hole with an offset of 5 mm from the centre of the wheel. This **must** be a tight fit on the motor shaft.

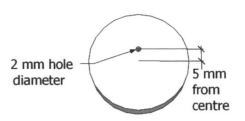

2 mm hole diameter

5 mm from centre

5. Push the motor shaft into the offset hole in the wheel. If it comes off in use you can glue it on. (But be careful not to get glue down the motor shaft as you can glue up the bearings and stop it turning.)

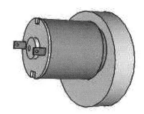

6. Clip the motor into the motor mount. Stick the motor mount firmly to the spacer using the glue gun or foam tape. Stick the spacer firmly to the end of the brush furthest from the handle. Check that the wheel can turn all the way round without touching the brush. If it touches the brush you need a thicker spacer.   Check there is a gap between the wheel and the spacer.

7. Use two cable ties to hold the motor firmly in place. If the cable ties aren't long enough you can join two together. Position the cable ties towards the back of the motor mount as shown. If you put them on the rounded end of the brush they tend to slide off.

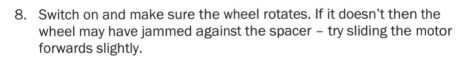

8. Switch on and make sure the wheel rotates. If it doesn't then the wheel may have jammed against the spacer – try sliding the motor forwards slightly.

9. If it still doesn't work then remove all the crocodile leads and hold the ends of the battery clip wires directly on the motor terminals to make sure the wheel rotates. If it doesn't your batteries may be flat. If it does, then re-introduce the crocodile leads one at a time, checking it still works.

10. Attach the battery holder and batteries firmly to the top of the brush using another cable tie as shown below. Place them as near the motor spacer as possible to balance the weight of the handle; otherwise if the handle is too heavy the brush can fall over.

11. Attach the toggle switch using two more cable ties as shown. Switch on and check the wheel still rotates, then switch off.

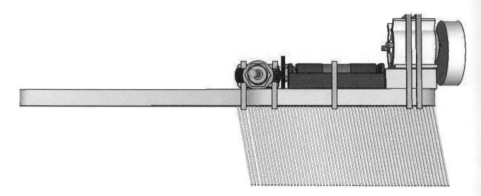

12. Tidy the crocodile leads by laying them neatly along the underside of the brush handle. Hold them in place with the remaining cable ties. Use the scissors to trim the ends of the cable ties.

13. Switch on, place the brush on a smooth level surface and watch it crawl along.

14. Using the glue gun or foam tape, decorate your brush with the eyes, pipe cleaners and feathers to make it look like a monster.

The wheel is mounted on an offset hole, so the centre of gravity keeps moving from side to side as it turns. This makes the brush vibrate.

The bristles are sloping, so when the brush tries to move one way due to the vibrations the bristles tend to dig in and prevent it. When it tries to move the other way the bristles slide easily across the surface. If you run the bristles over the palm of your hand you can feel them sliding easily one way but not the other.

Electric buggy

You will need:

- Battery holder with two AA batteries fitted
- Battery clip
- Toggle switch
- Motor and motor mount
- 3 crocodile leads
- 4 mm thick corrugated cardboard or corrugated plastic, e.g. Corriflute
- 2 small matching bottle tops about 2.5 to 3 cm diameter, e.g. from a Tetrapack juice carton. Smaller bottle tops will make your buggy go faster and larger ones will make it go slower.
- 4 plastic milk bottle tops
- 2 wooden skewers (preferably bamboo)
- 2 plastic drinking straws
- Stretchy rubber band ~ 1 mm thick x 1 mm wide x 6 cm long
- 3 more rubber bands (3 cm to 6 cm long)
- Small teddy bear or similar
- Glue gun or double sided tape and double sided foam tape
- Large lump of Blu Tack
- Large scissors or secateurs (younger readers should ask a responsible adult to help them)
- Ruler and pencil or felt tip pen
- Pencil sharpener
- Responsible adult with a Stanley knife
- Optional – 2 large cable ties (e.g. 20 cm long)

1. Mark out a rectangular chassis on the corrugated cardboard or plastic as shown on the right.

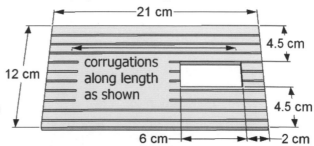

2. Ask a responsible adult to cut the chassis out for you using the Stanley knife. If you don't have one you could use a large pair of scissors for the outside of the chassis and a pair of nail scissors to cut the slot.

3. Cut one 13 cm length and two 6 cm lengths of plastic drinking straw. Attach the 13 cm length near the back of the chassis as shown, using the glue gun or foam tape.

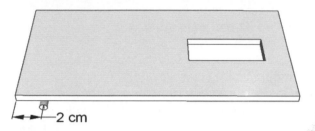

└─►├─2 cm

4. Support each of the bottle tops on the Blu Tack and pierce a hole in it using the sharp end of a skewer as shown on the right. Take out the Blu Tack.

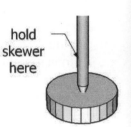

hold skewer here

5. Sharpen the blunt end of each skewer using the pencil sharpener.

6. Slide the two small bottle tops onto the skewer from opposite ends, with the open ends facing out as shown below. Stick them together firmly using the glue gun or double sided tape to make the 'pulley'.

7. Slide the stretchy rubber band over the pulley.

8. Slide the two 6 cm lengths of straw onto the ends of the skewer.

9. Place the pulley assembly on the chassis as shown and mark the position of the straws using the pencil or felt tip pen. The pulley needs to be near the end of the slot, but not touching it.

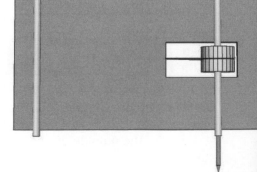

10. Glue the straws onto the chassis in the position you marked. This is quite tricky and you may need some help. Be careful not to get glue on the skewer as it needs to turn freely.

11. Spin the pulley assembly and make sure it rotates freely in the straws.

12. Clip the motor into the motor mount and loop the rubber band over the motor shaft. Follow the sequence in the picture below to position the motor and tension the rubber band.

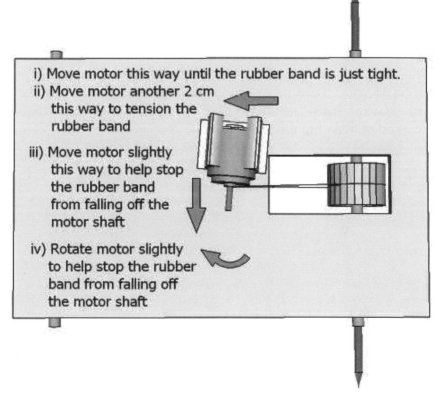

i) Move motor this way until the rubber band is just tight.
ii) Move motor another 2 cm this way to tension the rubber band
iii) Move motor slightly this way to help stop the rubber band from falling off the motor shaft
iv) Rotate motor slightly to help stop the rubber band from falling off the motor shaft

13. Mark the position of the motor mount on the chassis by drawing round it.

14. Remove the rubber band from the motor shaft and stick the motor mount (with motor clipped in) onto the chassis in the position you marked, using glue or foam tape.

15. Make the following circuit and check that it works. Refer to section 1 of the coloured spinning disc project on pages 3-4 for more details of how to do this.

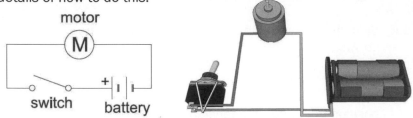

16. Loop the rubber band over the motor shaft and switch on. Check the skewer goes round and the rubber band doesn't fall off. If it does then adjust the motor position. If the motor mount comes loose you could make holes in the chassis on either side and attach it firmly with cable ties.

17. Stick the battery holder and switch onto the chassis in a position where the crocodile leads will not touch the bottle tops or the stretchy rubber band.

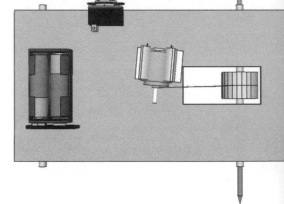

18. Design a seat for the teddy out of corrugated cardboard, corrugated plastic or folded card. Stick it towards the rear of the chassis – it could go on top of the battery holder. You can use the remaining rubber band as a seat belt.

19. Slide the second skewer though the drinking straw on the back of the chassis. Being careful not to pierce your fingers, press the four milk bottle tops onto the skewers with the open ends facing out.

20. Make sure the 'wheels' (bottle tops) at the back rotate freely. If they don't, make sure they are not rubbing against the chassis. Switch on and make sure the front wheels rotate and are not rubbing or glued in position.

21. Test your buggy on a smooth flat surface. You can try different sized wheels to make it go faster or slower. Once you are happy with your wheels snip off the sharp ends of the skewers using the large scissors or secateurs. Younger readers should ask a responsible adult to help them.

If you use a bigger diameter 'pulley' (pair of bottle tops) the buggy goes slower, assuming you use the same sized wheels. If you use a smaller diameter pulley the buggy goes faster.

As you can see below, for a pulley ten times as big as the motor shaft it takes ten turns of the motor to give one turn of the pulley. If the pulley is only five times as big it only takes five turns of the motor to turn the pulley once.

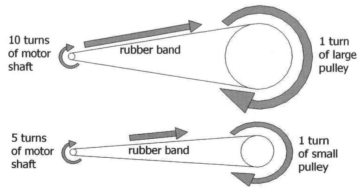

10 turns of motor shaft — rubber band — 1 turn of large pulley

5 turns of motor shaft — rubber band — 1 turn of small pulley

If you make the pulley too small you may overload the motor and make it stall (stop going round). You must then switch it off or it can get too hot and 'burn out'.

Paddle boat

You will need:

- Battery holder with two AA batteries fitted
- Battery clip
- Toggle switch
- Motor/worm gearbox (two versions of this are shown on page 2)
- 3 crocodile leads
- 2 small rubber bands (2 cm to 5 cm long)
- 2 small plastic bags e.g. sandwich bags or smaller
- 4 large polystyrene foam pizza bases
- Coca Cola, Diet Coke or Coke Zero aluminium drinks can
- 2 wine corks (preferably plastic)
- 2 push map drawing pins
- Felt tip pen and ruler
- Responsible adult with a Stanley knife
- Sharp scissors
- Glue gun or double sided foam tape and sticky tape e.g. Sellotape
- Drill and 3 mm or 4 mm drill bit (3 mm for the clip-in motor/gearbox or 4 mm for the screw mounted version)
- Vice or clamp
- Mug 8 cm in diameter

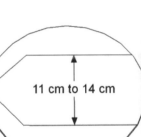

push map drawing pin

Also, if using the screw mounted motor gearbox:

- Motor mount
- 2 more wine corks (preferably plastic)
- 4 mm diameter wooden rod and secateurs

11 cm to 14 cm

1. Use the felt tip pen and ruler to mark out a boat shape on one of the pizza bases. Make it 11 cm to 14 cm wide and use the whole length of the pizza base, as shown above right. Cut it out using the sharp scissors, or ask a responsible adult with a Stanley knife to cut it out for you.

2. Use this boat shape as a template to draw two more boat shapes and cut these out as well. Stick the boat shapes together using glue or foam tape all the way round. Try to make sure there are no gaps for the water to get in.

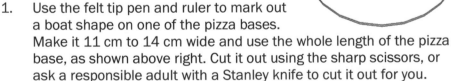

3. Use the felt tip pen and ruler to mark out a square 10 cm x 10 cm on the remaining pizza base. Cut it out and use it as a template to make another one. If using the clip-in motor/gearbox make a third one. Stick them to each other and to the boat as shown.

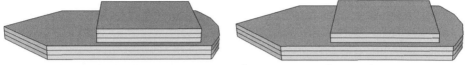

Clip-in motor/gearbox version   Screw mounted motor/gearbox version

4. Make the following circuit - refer to section 1 of the coloured spinning disc project on pages 3-4 for more details of how to do this. Switch it on and make sure that the motor/worm gearbox shaft turns, then switch off. Sometimes the screw mounted motor/gearbox jams, in which case you may need to loosen the screws slightly.

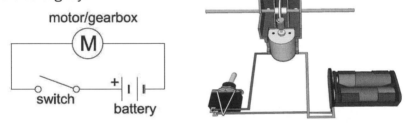

motor/gearbox

M

switch

+ battery

5. Make sure the gearbox shaft is turning forwards, as shown on the right. If it is turning backwards then swap over the crocodile clips on the back of the motor. If you are using the screw-mounted motor/gearbox clip it into the motor mount as shown.

6. Clamp two of the corks in turn in the vice and drill a hole half way through each the same diameter as the motor/gearbox shaft (clip-in version 3 mm, screw mounted version 4 mm). They must be a tight fit on the shaft.

7. Ask a responsible adult to cut the top 2 cm and the bottom 1.2 cm off the aluminium drinks can using the Stanley knife. Throw away the ends – these can be sharp.

 It is very important not to use a steel can, e.g. a baked bean can. These can be extremely sharp.

8.	Slit the can along its length using the scissors and flatten it out. Using the mug as a template, draw and cut two 8 cm diameter discs from the sides of the coke can using the large scissors. Throw away any trimmings as they can be spikey.

9.	If you are using the screw mounted motor/gearbox, drill a 4 mm hole all the way through the two remaining corks. Use the secateurs to cut two 4 cm lengths of the 4 mm diameter wooden rod. Younger readers should ask a responsible adult to help them use the secateurs. Use the rod to assemble each pair of corks as shown. 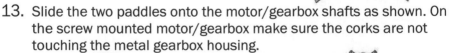 join corks with rod

10.	Place the aluminium discs on a table and stick one of the corks or corks assemblies to each of them with the hole at the top as shown. If using a glue gun put the glue on the cork, rather than the aluminium. This is because aluminium is a very good conductor of heat, so the glue could cool down and set before you have time to stick the parts together. Hold the cork, not the disc, to avoid burning your fingers.

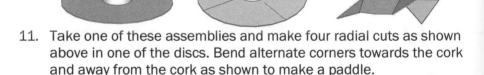

11.	Take one of these assemblies and make four radial cuts as shown above in one of the discs. Bend alternate corners towards the cork and away from the cork as shown to make a paddle.

12.	Take the other cork/disc assembly and make a mirror image of the paddle you just made.

13.	Slide the two paddles onto the motor/gearbox shafts as shown. On the screw mounted motor/gearbox make sure the corks are not touching the metal gearbox housing.

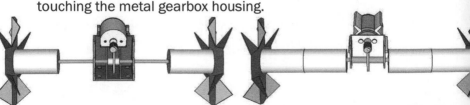

Clip-in motor/gearbox   Screw mounted motor/gearbox

14. Rest the boat on the mug. Stick the motor/gearbox and paddle assembly onto it as shown. Make sure the paddles do not touch the edge of the boat.

15. Put the battery holder and the switch into the two small plastic bags with the wires sticking out. You can trim the plastic bags to make them look neater. Then seal them with sticky tape to prevent the water getting in.

16. Place the batteries on the raised platform as shown below. Balance the boat on the side of your hand and adjust the position of the batteries until the centre of gravity is roughly in the middle. Place the switch somewhere accessible on the platform, and stick the switch and batteries in position.
Press the push map drawing pins through the paddles into the ends of the corks as shown to help keep the paddles on,

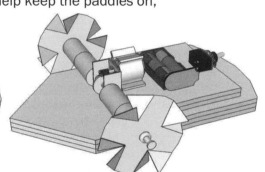

Clip-in motor/gearbox   Screw mounted motor/gearbox

17. Try out your paddle boat on water. If it turns to one side then you can try adjusting the shape of the paddles or moving them in or out along the motor/gearbox shaft slightly. If the paddles slip on the shafts you can glue the corks onto the shafts.

Steel is roughly three times denser than aluminium (i.e. the same volume weighs three times more) and three times as stiff. Aluminium is also much softer than steel and drinks cans are made of very thin material, which is why you can cut them with a pair of scissors and easily bend them to shape.

Cereal racer

You will need:

- Battery holder with two AA batteries fitted
- Battery clip
- Toggle switch
- Motor/worm gearbox (two versions of this are shown on page 2)
- 3 crocodile leads
- Small rubber band (2 cm to 5 cm long)
- Empty mini cereal box (e.g. from a variety pack)
- 4 plastic milk bottle tops
- Wooden skewer (preferably bamboo)
- Plastic drinking straw
- Sticky tape e.g. Sellotape
- Insulating tape
- Sharp pencil and large lump of Blu Tack
- Large scissors or secateurs
- Ruler and biro
- Pencil sharpener.
- Sharp nail scissors

1. Make the following circuit - refer to section 1 of the coloured spinning disc project on pages 3-4 for more details of how to do this. Make sure the insulating sleeves are covering the crocodile clips to avoid short circuits. Use the rubber band to stop the crocodile clips falling off the switch.

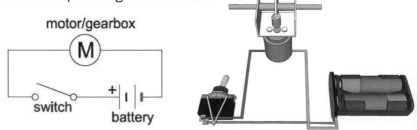

2. Switch on and make sure that the motor/worm gearbox shaft turns, then switch off. Sometimes the screw mounted motor/gearbox jams, in which case you may need to loosen the screws slightly.

3. Tape up the lid of the cereal box.

4. Use the ruler and biro to carefully mark out pairs of hole positions on the front and back of the cereal box. These are the crosses shown on the right.

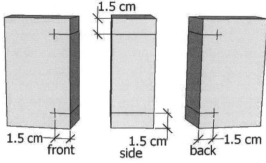

front   side   back

5. Use the sharp pencil to pierce the four holes you marked out.

6. Support each of the milk bottle tops on the Blu Tack and pierce with the skewer as shown on the right. Take out the Blu Tack.

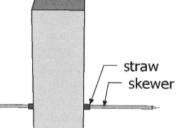

hold skewer here

7. Use the ruler and biro to mark a 5 cm length on the drinking straw. Use the sharp pencil to enlarge the pair of holes at the bottom of the cereal box until the drinking straw slides though. Push the drinking straw through both holes as shown on the right and cut it off at the 5 cm mark.

8. Sharpen the blunt end of the skewer using the pencil sharpener and slide it through the middle of the drinking straw as shown on the right.

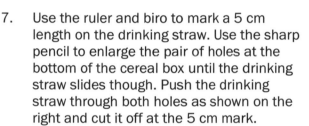

straw
skewer

9. Push two of the milk bottle tops onto the ends of the skewers with the open ends facing out. Slide the bottle tops along the skewer until they are just touching the ends of the straw.

 Be careful not to pierce your fingers with the skewer when pushing on the bottle tops.

10. Move the bottle tops apart very slightly, then spin them and make sure the skewer rotates freely in the straw. Trim off the ends of the skewer using the large scissors or secateurs. Younger readers should ask a responsible adult to help them use the secateurs.

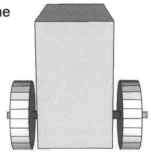

11. Use the ruler and biro to mark a hole in the side of the cereal box, 1.5 cm from the bottom as shown. Pierce the hole with the sharp pencil, then use the sharp nail scissors to enlarge it to 1.2 cm diameter to fit the toggle switch.

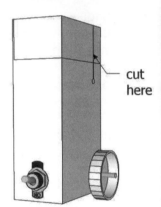

1.2 cm hole

1.5 cm

12. Enlarge the remaining pair of holes at the top of the cereal box using the sharp pencil, until you can slide the motor/worm gearbox shaft in easily from the outside.

13. Take the tape off and open the top of the cereal box. Cut a slit from the edge to one of the holes on the side as shown. Repeat for the hole on the other side.

cut here

14. Unscrew the nut and remove the on-off label from the toggle switch (if fitted). Push the threaded part of the switch through the 1.2 cm hole from the inside, then put back the on-off label (if fitted) and screw the nut on firmly.

15. Remove the second rubber band holding the crocodile leads to the wires from the battery clip. Wrap a strip of insulating tape around the backs of the crocodile clips on the back of the motor to hold them together. Make a small loop with the leads and tape them onto the top of the motor. This is to stop the clips falling off the motor terminals.

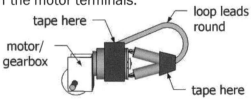

tape here

loop leads round

motor/ gearbox

tape here

16. Slide the motor/gearbox along the cut into the cereal packet until the shaft is sticking out of the pair of holes as shown.

17. Switch on and check the motor/gearbox shaft still turns. Switch off again.

18. Cut a strip of insulating tape and lay it down sticky side up. Place the end of the red wire to the battery clip and the crocodile clip attached to it on the tape as shown. Wrap the tape around the connection to hold it securely.

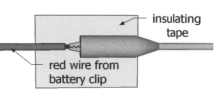

insulating tape

red wire from battery clip

19. Repeat step 18 for the black wire to the battery clip.

20. Slide the battery holder into the cereal box as shown so that it butts up against the switch and carefully push in the crocodile leads. Switch on and check the motor/gearbox shaft still goes round, then switch off.

21. Sellotape up the top of the cereal box.

22. Push the two remaining bottle tops over the two ends of the motor/gearbox shaft. You may need to enlarge the holes with the sharp pencil. Don't enlarge them too much as they need to be a tight fit on the shaft. Make sure the bottle tops are not touching the cereal packet so that they can turn freely. Now try out your cereal racer.

A motor/worm gearbox is used to reduce speed. The 'worm', similar to a screw, is mounted on the motor shaft. The worm turns the 'wheel' which is mounted on the output shaft. Each turn of the worm moves the wheel round by 1 tooth. If there are 40 teeth on the wheel then 40 turns of the motor will only rotate the output shaft once.

motor

worm

wheel

output shaft

Chair-o-plane

You will need:

- Battery holder with two AA batteries fitted
- Battery clip
- Toggle switch
- Motor
- Motor mount
- 3 crocodile leads
- Pulley 4 cm to 5 cm in diameter
- 25 cm long wooden rod to fit the pulley (normally 4 or 5 mm in diameter)

pulley

- Stretchy rubber band ~ 1 mm thick x 1.5 mm wide x 3 to 4 cm long
- Wine cork (preferably plastic)
- Piece of cardboard about 1 mm thick
- Old plastic drinks bottle with lid (Tropicana 330 ml or similar)
- 2 old CDs
- Plastic pot about 12 cm in diameter x 4 cm high
- 3 stones about 3 cm x 3 cm x 3 cm
- Old cereal box
- 4 to 8 small Lego men or similar weighing about 4 g each
- 2 small rubber bands (2 cm to 5 cm long)
- Large cable tie
- Pencil and ruler
- Sharp scissors
- Drill and set of drill bits 4 mm to 6 mm in diameter
- Glue gun
- Vice and bradawl
- Sticky tape e.g. Sellotape

1. Make the following circuit and check that it works. Refer to section 1 of the coloured spinning disc project on pages 3-4 for more details of how to do this. Unclip the crocodile leads from the back of the motor.

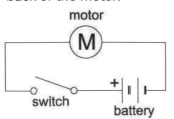

motor

(M)

switch

+ | | |

battery

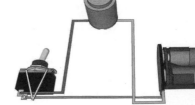

2. Turn the plastic pot upside down, place it on the card, draw round it and cut out the disc to make a lid (unless the pot already has a lid). Stick the stones into the plastic pot using the glue gun and plenty of glue, then glue on the lid.

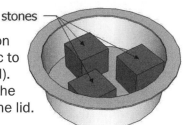

stones

3. Clamp the cork in the vice and drill a hole straight through the middle with the same diameter as the wooden rod. It may be easier to keep the hole straight if you use a smaller drill first. The cork must be a tight fit on the rod. If it is too tight to push on then re-drill the hole.

4. Use the bradawl to pierce a hole in centre of the lid of the bottle and another in the bottom. You may need the help of a competent adult. Drill out the holes; they need to be slightly larger in diameter than the wooden rod, so that the rod can turn easily. Check the rod is a loose fit in the holes.

hole → ← hole

5. Turn the plastic pot upside down and stick a CD on the top.

6. Stick the bottle in the middle of the CD and the battery holder and switch on either side as shown on the right.

7. Slide the rod down through the two holes in the bottle until it rests on the plastic container.

8. Use the pencil to mark the rod 2 mm above the bottle top.

mark pencil line here

9. Take the rod out and clamp it in the vice. Push the pulley down to the pencil mark as shown below.

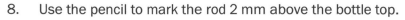

pencil mark —

10. Slide the cork onto the rod and stick it to the top of the pulley as shown on the right.

11. Slide the rod back into the holes in the bottle.

12. Clip the motor into the motor mount.

13. Stick the motor mount onto the side of the lid as shown on the right, so that the motor shaft is the same height as the middle of the pulley.

14. Use the cable tie to hold the motor and mount firmly in place as shown below right.

15. Stretch the rubber band on the pulley over the motor shaft.

16. Re-attach the crocodile clips to the motor contacts. They should be vertical as shown; this is so that they won't get in the way when the chair-o-plane rotates. Switch on, make sure the rod rotates then switch off.

17. Tidy the crocodile leads neatly at the bottom, tie them up with the second rubber band and rest them on the CD. Make sure the crocodile clips and leads will not get in the way when the chairs rotate. Switch on and check it still works, then switch off.

18. Cut a 4 cm diameter disc out of the cardboard. Being careful not to cut your fingers, pierce a hole in the middle of the disc using one blade of the sharp scissors. Rotate the blade in the hole to enlarge it so that it will just fit onto the rod.

19. Slide the card disc over the top of the rod and glue it onto the cork.

20. Using the glue gun, stick the second CD to the top of the card disc as shown on the right, making sure the holes in the middle line up.

21. Cut a 1 cm x 24 cm strip of the cereal box for each Lego man.

22. Bend the strips into long triangular shapes, Sellotape the tops together as shown and slide in the Lego men. If you don't have any Lego men you can make figures out of cardboard instead.

23. Cut a seat back 1.5 cm high and a safety strap 0.5 cm high for each Lego man as shown and tape on.

Sellotape together

24. Use a strip of Sellotape to attach each of the chairs to the outside of the top CD as shown below right. They must be evenly spaced to minimise vibrations.

25. Switch on and try out your chair-o-plane. If the Lego men are going backwards then switch off and swap over the crocodile clips attached to the motor contacts.

26. If the rubber band comes off the motor shaft during running, slide the motor up slightly so that the rubber band runs near the bottom of the shaft.

Sellotape

When the chair-o-plane rotates the Lego men fly out because of something called 'centrifugal force'. The Lego men are trying to go in a straight line but they are attached to the spinning CD, forcing them to go round in a circle. So they fly out as far as they can.

Lighthouse

You will need:

- Battery holder with two AA batteries fitted
- Battery clip
- Toggle switch
- Motor/worm gearbox (two versions of this are shown on page 2)
- Lamp holder with 3V lamp fitted
- 5 crocodile leads
- Small rubber band
- 3 old CDs
- A one litre transparent plastic squash bottle with label removed
- 2 large (500g) yoghourt pots
- A two litre plastic drinks bottle
- Large sheet of white card (A3 or bigger)
- A3 sheet of red or black card (or two A4 sheets)
- Sheet of thick card (0.5 mm to 1 mm thick)
- Coca Cola, Diet Coke or Coke Zero aluminium drinks can
- Wine cork (preferably plastic)
- Ruler and pencil
- Scissors and sharp nail scissors
- Vice and drill with 3 mm, 4 mm and 5 mm drill bits
- Transparent sticky tape e.g. Sellotape
- Glue gun or double sided foam sticky tape
- Responsible adult with a Stanley knife

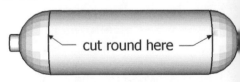

1. Drill a 5 mm hole in the centre of one of the yoghourt pots, then stick it to the second yoghourt pot as shown using the glue gun or double sided foam sticky tape.

2. Stick one end of this assembly to the middle of a CD.

3. Use the sharp nail scissors to cut the top and bottom off the two litre drinks bottle.

— cut round here —

4. Slide the cylindrical length of drinks bottle down over the yoghourt pot assembly until it rests on the CD.

5. Stick the second CD onto the other end of the assembly.

6. Cut the large sheet of white card to the height of the two yoghourt pots (probably about 24.5 cm) as shown below, and Sellotape one end onto the section of drinks bottle. Wrap the card around the drinks bottle and Sellotape up the seam.

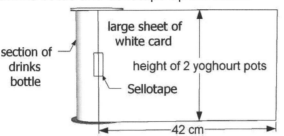

7. Cut three strips of red or black card about 5 cm wide x 42 cm long. Wrap them around the white card as shown and tape them in place. If you have A4 sheets you will need to join on an extra piece of card. You have now finished the 'tower'.

8. Make the following circuit - refer to section 4 of the paddle boat project on page 27 for more details of how to do this. If using the screw mounted motor/gearbox turn it on its side, rest the end of the shaft on a hard surface, e.g. a chopping board, and press down until the shaft slides through, as shown below right.

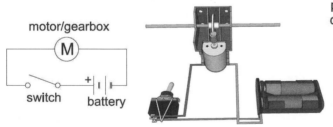

Screw mounted
motor/gearbox ONLY

9. Leaving the circuit connected, stick the motor/gearbox housing onto the CD as shown. If using the clip-in motor/gearbox slide one end of the shaft into the hole in the yoghourt pot. The two crocodile leads onto the motor contacts should be connected in the orientation shown.

10. Stick the battery housing and switch onto the CD as shown. Tidy the crocodile leads neatly and tape them to the top of the CD.

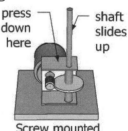
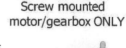

11. Switch on and make sure the motor/gearbox shaft rotates, then switch off. Rest the lamp holder on the battery housing.

12. Take the fourth crocodile lead and clip one end to a terminal on the lamp holder and the other end to the nose of the crocodile clip attached to the black wire from the battery clip. Take the fifth crocodile lead and clip one end to the free lamp holder terminal and the other end to the **same** switch terminal to which the motor/gearbox is connected.

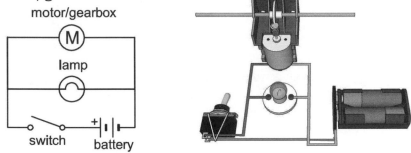

13. Switch on and make sure the motor/gearbox shaft rotates and the lamp comes on. Tidy the wires neatly and tape them down.

14. Place the third CD on the thick card and draw round it. Mark the hole centres as shown below. You can use the central hole in the CD as a template to draw the 1.6 cm diameter hole. Cut out the disc and use the sharp nail scissors to cut the two holes.

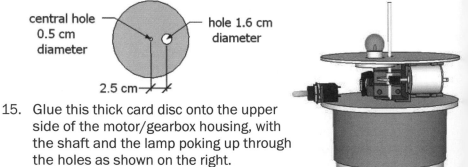

15. Glue this thick card disc onto the upper side of the motor/gearbox housing, with the shaft and the lamp poking up through the holes as shown on the right.

16. Cut the following strip from the remains of the white card.

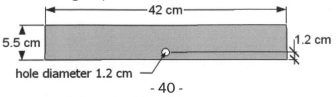

17. Push the hole in the strip over the switch. Wrap the strip around the upper CD and thick card disc as shown on the right and tape it in place. This part is the 'gallery'.

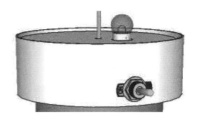

Type of motor/gearbox	H	H - 2	D
	7.5 cm	5.5 cm	3 mm
	6.0 cm	4.0 cm	4 mm

Table 1 - Dimensions for alternative types of motor/gearbox

18. Clamp the cork in the vice and drill a hole straight through the middle the same diameter D as the motor/gearbox shaft (see Table 1 above). The cork must be a tight fit on the shaft. If it is too tight to push on then re-drill the hole.

19. Use the sharp nail scissors to cut the top off the one litre squash bottle to leave the bottom H cm (see Table 1). Turn it upside down as shown here.

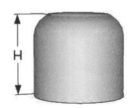

20. Cut the shape below from the remaining white card (see Table 1 for dimensions). Stick it round the section of squash bottle as shown on the right. This will be the 'lantern room'.

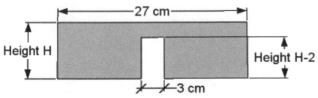

21. Stick the cork firmly to the inside of the squash bottle, in the middle, as shown on the right.

22. Ask a responsible adult to cut the top and bottom 2 cm off the aluminium drinks can using the Stanley knife. Throw away the ends; they can be sharp.

 It is very important not to use a steel can, e.g. a baked bean can. These can be extremely sharp.

23. Slit the coke can lengthways using the scissors, then trim it to the height shown. Throw away any trimmings as they can be spikey.

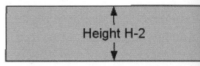

Height H-2

24. Stick the rectangle to the inside of the lantern room as shown to act as a reflector. Put the gap in the same orientation as the cutout in the white card. If using a glue gun be careful not to burn your fingers; aluminium is a very good conductor of heat!

reflector

25. Position the cork on the end of the motor/ gearbox shaft and slide the lantern room down until it is just clear of the card disc. Switch on and check the lantern room rotates and the light comes on.

26. Place the third CD on the remaining red or black card and draw round it. Cut out the disc and then cut a segment out of it as shown on the right.

27. Bend this into a cone, tape up the seam and stick it to the top of the lantern room.

28. Try out your lighthouse in a dark room.

 *In traditional lighthouses the light does not flash on and off. It stays on continuously and a series of lenses and a parabolic (dish) reflector rotate around it, focussing the light into a powerful beam which can be seen for many miles. The light appears to flash as the beam sweeps past.*

Motorbike

You will need:

- Battery holder with two AA batteries fitted
- Battery clip
- Toggle switch
- Motor/worm gearbox (two versions of this are shown on page 2)
- Motor mount (if using the screw mounted motor/gearbox)
- 3 crocodile leads
- Small rubber band
- Square wooden rod 1 cm x 1 cm x 80 cm
- Wooden skewer (preferably bamboo)
- 4 old CDs
- 4 'penny' washers about 40 mm in diameter
- 2 M6 or M8 nylon washers (or metal if you don't have nylon ones)
- 10 cm length of 3 mm diameter aluminium wire (or use a wooden skewer)
- Wine cork (preferably plastic)
- Soft toy to ride the motorbike
- 5 cable ties (approximately 20 cm long)
- Sheet of black A4 card
- Hand drill with 3 mm and 4 mm drill bits
- Glue gun and black insulating tape
- Pencil and ruler
- Hacksaw
- G-clamp or vice
- Sandpaper
- Secateurs
- Black marker pen
- Silver spray (optional)
- Silver card (optional)
- Scissors

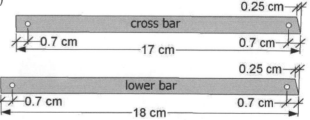

1. Mark out and cut the wooden rod as shown above right.

2. Drill the 3 mm diameter holes as shown. Tape the two uprights together before drilling, so that the holes line up. Do the same with the two front forks. Remove the tape after drilling.

3. Smooth with sandpaper. You can also use sandpaper to make the sloping ends on the cross bar and lower bar. Rub down all the edges of the front forks with sandpaper to round them off.

4. If you have silver spray, spray the front forks and the sloping end of both the cross bar and lower bar, then leave to dry.

5. Cut five 3.5 cm long pieces of skewer using the secateurs.

6. Assemble the frame as shown below. The skewer should be a tight push fit in the holes (but not so tight it won't go in!)

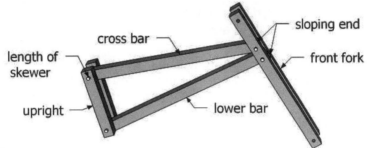

sloping end

cross bar

length of skewer

front fork

upright

lower bar

Try holding the uprights and changing the slope of the front forks – you will notice that the frame is flexible. You have just made what is known as a 'four bar mechanism'. If the frame was a triangle it would be rigid, but having a fourth member allows it to move. Some mountain bikes use a four bar mechanism for their rear wheel suspension.

7. Make the following circuit - refer to section 4 of the paddle boat project on page 27 for more details of how to do this.

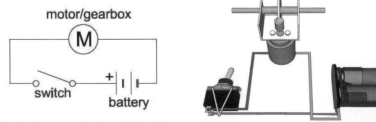

motor/gearbox

M

switch

+ battery

8. Switch on and check that the motor/ worm gearbox shaft turns in the direction shown on the right. If it turns the other way then swap over the crocodile clips on the back of the motor.

9. If you are using the screw mounted motor/gearbox, clip it into the motor mount. Attach the motor/gearbox, switch and battery box firmly to the frame using cable ties as shown on the right. Fold the leads neatly and attach them to the frame as well using the remaining cable tie. Trim the ends of the cable ties.

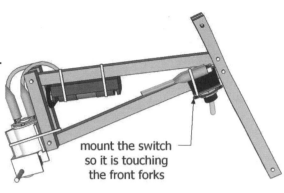

mount the switch so it is touching the front forks

10. Take the 4 old CDs and use the marker pen to draw tyres and spokes on the shiny silver side as shown on the right.

penny washer

11. Glue or tape on the penny washers as shown, making sure the hole centres line up.

12. Stick two of the CDs together with the penny washers on the outside. Then stick the M6 or M8 washers on either side as shown below, making sure the hole centres line up, to make the front wheel.

CD   nylon (or metal) washer

13. Slide the front wheel in between the front forks and push the remaining 3.5 cm length of skewer through the holes at the bottom of the forks and through the middle of the front wheel to hold it in place.

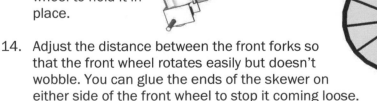

14. Adjust the distance between the front forks so that the front wheel rotates easily but doesn't wobble. You can glue the ends of the skewer on either side of the front wheel to stop it coming loose.

15. Drill a hole through the middle of the cork the same diameter as the motor/gearbox shaft (4 mm for the screw mounted motor/gearbox and 3 mm for the clip-in version).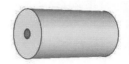

16. Cut 1.5 cm off one end of the cork. You can use the hacksaw or ask a responsible adult with a Stanley knife to cut it for you. Glue the uncut surface to the non-decorated side of a CD as shown below, making sure the hole centres line up.

17. Repeat step 16 for the other end of the cork and the final CD.

18. Slide one cork assembly onto each end of the motor/gearbox output shaft. Make sure they do not touch the motor/gearbox housing, so that the wheel can turn easily. Switch on and try out the motorbike, then switch off.

19. Poke the 3 mm aluminium wire through the two holes at the top of the front forks. Curve it to look like handlebars as shown above. If you don't have aluminium wire you can use a 10 cm length of wooden skewer instead to make straight handlebars. Wrap black insulating tape round the ends of the handlebars to look like grips.

20. Cut out the following shape from the sheet of A4 black card. This will be the bodywork. Fold up all the edge flaps marked 'a' along the dotted lines, then flatten them again.

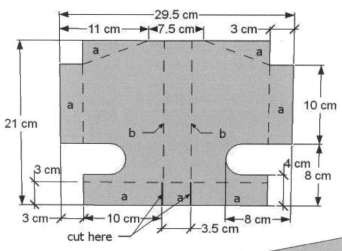

21. Fold up the two sides along the dotted lines marked 'b' above. Slide the bodywork down over the frame as shown. Fold the pairs of 'a' flaps over each other and stick them together.

22. You can add an engine, gearbox and exhaust pipe made from the silver card as shown, marked up using the marker pen. Bend the exhaust pipe outwards so that it doesn't rub against the back wheel; you may need some extra card to stiffen it at the bend.

23. You can also make a seat out of spare card for your soft toy so that it doesn't fall off.

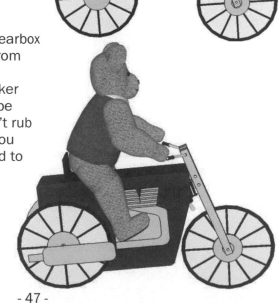

Autorickshaw

You will need:

- Battery holder with two AA batteries fitted
- Battery clip
- Toggle switch
- Motor/worm gearbox (two versions of this are shown on page 2)
- Motor mount (if using the screw mounted motor/gearbox)
- Lamp holder with 3V lamp fitted
- 5 crocodile leads
- 2 small rubber bands (2 cm to 5 cm long)
- 4 mm thick corrugated plastic or cardboard for the base (alternatively you could use an upside down, **well washed,** plastic chicken tray, as used for selling whole chickens in supermarkets)
- 3 mm thick corrugated cardboard or black corrugated plastic
- Black poster paint (if using cardboard)
- A4 sheet of bright yellow card
- A4 sheet of light yellow or black card
- 4 plastic milk bottle tops (3 if using the clip-in motor/gearbox)
- Length of old bicycle inner tube (size 26" x 1.75")
- Wooden skewer and drinking straw
- Transparent plastic sheet (e.g. from a cake or biscuit display box)
- Glue gun or double sided tape
- Large lump of Blu Tack
- Sharp scissors or secateurs (younger readers should ask a responsible adult to help them use the secateurs)
- Ruler and pencil
- Stapler, pencil sharpener and sticky tape e.g. Sellotape
- Responsible adult with a craft knife

1. Mark out and cut the sides of the autorickshaw from the 3 mm thick corrugated plastic or cardboard as shown below. If you do not have a strip long enough you can join two strips together using the stapler. If using a chicken tray you may need a longer strip than this to go all the way round.

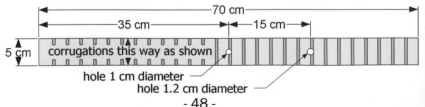

2. To make the holes, pierce the strip with one of the scissor blades and rotate the blade in the hole to enlarge it. Push the bulb into the central hole as shown below.

bulb in bulb holder ⟶   ⟵ switch

3. Unscrew the nut from the switch and remove the on/off label (if fitted). Push the threaded part of the switch through the second hole as shown above, then replace the on/off label and screw the nut on firmly.

4. If using the screw mounted motor/gearbox make the base shown here from the 4 mm thick corrugated cardboard or plastic.

|←——————22 cm——————→|

corrugations
this way
⟵⟶

14 cm

hole 1 cm
diameter

|←—7 cm—→|

5. If using the clip-in motor/gearbox mark out the base and wheel mount below instead. Ask a responsible adult with a craft knife to cut it out for you. Use the glue gun or double sided tape to stick the wheel mount to the bottom of the base as shown.

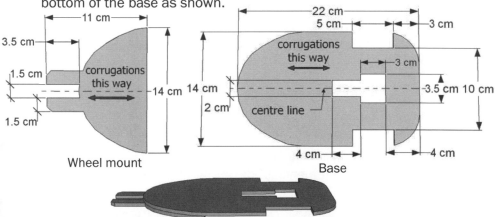

|←——11 cm——→|

3.5 cm ←→

1.5 cm

corrugations
this way
⟵⟶

1.5 cm

14 cm   14 cm

Wheel mount

|←——————22 cm——————→|
|←——5 cm——→| ⟵→ ⟵ 3 cm

corrugations
this way
⟵⟶

⟵→ 3 cm

2 cm   centre line

3.5 cm   10 cm

4 cm ←→   ⟵→ 4 cm

Base

6. Stick the sides around the base as shown below. Overlap and staple the back. If using cardboard paint black and leave to dry.

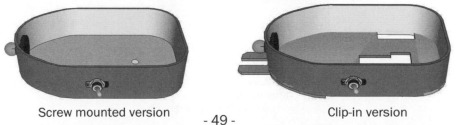

Screw mounted version   Clip-in version

- 49 -

7. Support each of the bottle tops on the Blu Tack and pierce a hole in it using the skewer as shown. Take out the Blu Tack.

8. Cut four 2 cm lengths of bicycle inner tube and stretch them around the milk bottle tops as tyres.

9. Push two of these 'wheels' onto the two ends of the motor/gearbox shaft. You may need to enlarge the holes slightly with the pencil. Don't enlarge them too much as they need to be a tight fit on the shaft.

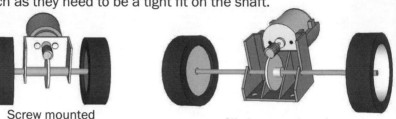

Screw mounted motor/gearbox

Clip-in motor/gearbox

10. If using the screw mounted motor/gearbox (otherwise go to 11):

i. Cut an 18 cm length of drinking straw. Sharpen the blunt end of the skewer using the pencil sharpener and slide it through the middle of the drinking straw.

ii. Being careful not to pierce your fingers, push the two remaining wheels onto the ends of the skewers with the open ends facing out.

iii. Slide the wheels along the skewer until they just touch the ends of the straw.

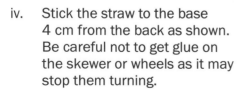

iv. Stick the straw to the base 4 cm from the back as shown. Be careful not to get glue on the skewer or wheels as it may stop them turning.

v. Move the wheels apart slightly, then spin them and make sure the skewer rotates freely in the straw. Trim off the ends of the skewer using the secateurs. Younger readers should ask a responsible adult to help them.

vi. Turn the motor mount upside down and clip it onto the motor as shown. Make sure the wheels are not touching the gearbox housing as this could stop them turning.

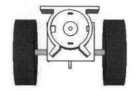

vii. Stick the motor mount onto the base as shown. Make sure the wheels are not touching the base.

11. If using the clip-in motor/gearbox (otherwise go to 12):

i. Being careful not to pierce your fingers, push the third wheel onto the skewer.

ii. Cut one 2 cm length and one 3 cm length of drinking straw. Slide them onto the skewer on either side of the wheel as shown.

2 cm length of straw — 3 cm length of straw
skewer — open end of bottle top

iii. Stick the lengths of straw to the underside of the wheel mount as shown. Be careful not to get glue on the skewer or bottle top as it may stop them turning. Spin the wheel and make sure the skewer rotates freely in the straw. Trim off the ends of the skewer using the secateurs. Younger readers should ask a responsible adult to help them.

iv. Slide the motor/gearbox up through the cut-out in the base then rotate into position as shown. You may need to adjust the position so that the wheels don't touch the base or the sides. Stick the plastic housing of the motor/gearbox to the base.

12. Place the battery holder inside the autorickshaw. Make the following circuit and check that it works. For the screw mounted motor/gearbox version feed one end of each of two crocodile leads through the hole in the base.

13. Make sure the autorickshaw moves forwards. If it moves backwards swap over the crocodile clips on the back of the motor.

14. Take the fourth crocodile lead and clip one end to a terminal on the lamp holder and the other end to the nose of the crocodile clip attached to the black wire from the battery clip. Take the fifth crocodile lead and clip one end to the free lamp holder terminal and the other end to the **same** switch terminal to which the motor/gearbox is connected.

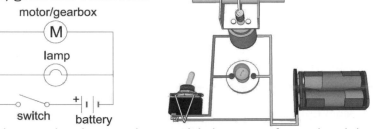

15. Switch on and make sure the autorickshaw goes forward and the light comes on.

In the circuit above the lamp and motor are connected in 'parallel'. You can try connecting them in series as follows:

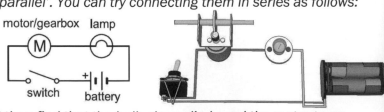

You should then find that the bulb glows dimly and the motor turns slowly, if at all. This is because the volts from the battery, which push the electricity round the circuit, are shared between the bulb and the motor. If you now connect them in parallel again both the bulb and the motor receive the full voltage and should work properly.

16. Cut the shape below left from the bright yellow card. Bend the top over as shown. Cut a 9 cm x 12 cm rectangle from the transparent plastic sheet and tape it to the card to make the windscreen.

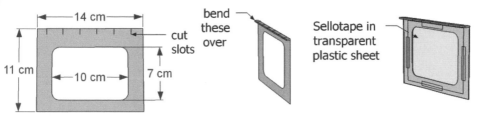

17. Make two 5 cm long cuts in the A4 light yellow or black card in the positions shown on the right to make the canopy.

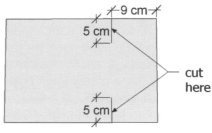

18. Cut a 2.5 cm wide strip of bright yellow card and stick it to the canopy as shown below.

19. Stick the windscreen to the front of the autorickshaw and the strip of card on the canopy to the back. Bend and staple the canopy as shown. Trim the sides and the front of the canopy so that it fits neatly over the top of the windscreen and stick it on.

20. You can make a seat for a teddy to ride in the autorickshaw – this also helps to cover up the wires. Don't stick it down as you may need access to change the batteries.

Paper dart launcher

You will need:

- Battery holder with two AA batteries fitted
- Battery clip
- Toggle switch
- 2 motors
- 5 crocodile leads
- 2 small rubber bands
- 3 mm to 4 mm thick hardboard (you may be able to buy this ready cut to size from your local builders merchant) or Foamex board (stiff foamed plastic used for making sign boards)
- 3 mm to 4 mm thick corrugated cardboard or plastic (e.g. Corriflute)
- 4 or more plastic milk bottle tops
- 3 cm length of old bicycle inner tube (size 26" x 1.75")
- Rubber band approximately 0.5 cm wide x 9 cm long
- Thin A4 sheet of coloured paper
- Sharp pencil and ruler
- Lump of Blu Tack
- Sharp scissors and sharp nail scissors
- Drill with 6 mm drill bit
- Hacksaw
- Sandpaper and wood saw (if using hardboard)
- Centre punch and hammer or small Phillips screwdriver
- Glue gun and glue sticks
- Responsible adult with a Stanley knife (if using Foamex board)

1. Mark out a rectangle as shown on the Foamex board or hardboard.

   25 cm
   2.5 cm 2 cm
   1 cm
   cut these slots
   4.2 cm
   2 holes 6 mm diameter 15
   cut these slots
   5.4 cm
   3.5 cm

2. If using Foamex board ask a responsible adult to cut it out for you; they can score the material deeply and then bend it along the score line to break it off.

3. If using hardboard you can cut it to size with the wood saw.

4. Mark out and cut the four slots in the sides using the hacksaw.

5. Carefully mark out, centre punch, then drill the holes – it is important to get the correct distance between the holes. If you don't have a centre punch then press hard with the small Phillips screwdriver to make an indent. If you are using hardboard then drill from the smooth side, sandpaper the rough side after drilling to remove the loose material, then drill back through from the rough side.

6. Push the front of the motors into the holes. If using hardboard push them in from the rough side. Rotate the motors until the connections on the back are oriented as shown.

7. Stretch the rubber band over the motors and hook it over the slots as shown. This is to help stop the motors coming out of the holes.

8. Use the sharp scissors to cut the back, two sides, motor retainer and cable retainer shown below from the corrugated cardboard or plastic.

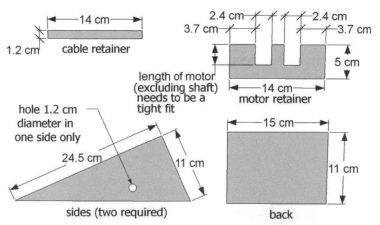

14 cm

1.2 cm   cable retainer

2.4 cm   2.4 cm
3.7 cm   3.7 cm

5 cm

length of motor
(excluding shaft)
needs to be a
tight fit

14 cm
motor retainer

hole 1.2 cm
diameter in
one side only

24.5 cm   11 cm

sides (two required)

15 cm

11 cm

back

9. Cut the 1.2 cm hole in one of the sides using the sharp nail scissors.

10. Slide the motor retainer over the back of the motors as shown and glue it to the base.

11. Glue the sides onto the base as shown. Then glue the back onto the sides and base and the battery holder to the base as shown.

12. Unscrew the nut from the switch and remove the metal on/off label (if fitted). Push the threaded part of the switch through the hole from the inside, then replace the on-off label and screw the nut on firmly.

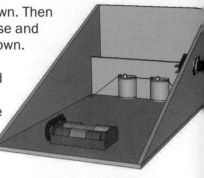

13. Connect one of the motors up to make the following circuit and check that it works. Refer to section 1 of the coloured spinning disc project on pages 3-4 for more details of how to do this.

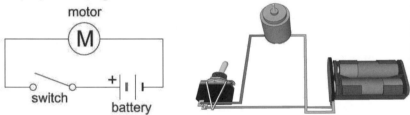

motor

M

switch

battery

14. Take the fourth crocodile lead and clip one end to a terminal on the second motor and the other end to the nose of the crocodile clip attached to the black wire from the battery clip. Take the fifth crocodile lead and clip one end to the free motor terminal and the other end to the **same** switch terminal to which the first motor is connected. The motors should now be connected in 'parallel' as shown.

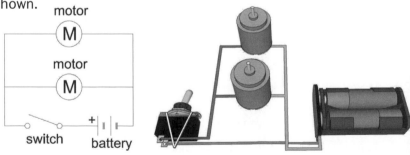

motor

M

motor

M

switch   battery

15. Turn the launcher over, switch on and check which way the motors turn. If they do not turn in the directions shown then swap over the connections on the backs of the motors, so that they do. Switch off again.

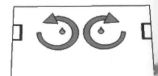

16. If the motors go round very slowly then you may have connected them in 'series'. Remove the crocodile leads and carefully follow the instructions given in sections 13 and 14.

17. Fold the loose crocodile leads up neatly. Slide in the cable retainer and glue it to the sides as shown to stop the leads falling out.

18. Support each of the bottle tops on the Blu Tack and pierce a small hole as near the centre as possible using the sharp pencil as shown. Don't make the hole too big as it must be a tight fit on the motor shaft. Take out the Blu Tack.

19. Cut two 9 mm strips of bicycle inner tube and stretch over the bottle tops as shown. Make sure the inner tube does not extend below the bottle top, so it won't rub on the base.

20. Slide the bottle tops onto the two motor shafts. Turn the bottle tops round by hand and see whether they move from side to side. If they do then use the spare bottle tops instead, being even more careful to get the holes in the middle!

21. Switch on and make sure the bottle tops go round. If they rub on the base slide them up the motor shafts slightly. If the mounting holes in the base are too close together the bottle tops may jam. If necessary re-drill the holes slightly further along the base. If the bottle tops come off in use put a bit of glue on the end of the motor shafts to hold them on.

22. Make this paper dart from half the thin A4 sheet of paper:

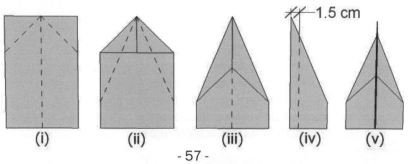

1.5 cm

(i) (ii) (iii) (iv) (v)

i) Fold in half lengthways then unfold. Fold in the top corners in the positions indicated by the dotted lines.

ii) Fold in the top corners again as indicated by the dotted lines.

iii) Fold in half lengthways.

iv) Fold one wing out to one side, and the other wing out to the other side, leaving a 1.5 cm strip for the body as indicated by the dotted line.

v) You should end up with the final shape (v) shown on page 57.

23. Switch on the paper dart launcher and place it on a table. Feed the paper dart in until the nose is caught by the two rotating wheels, then let go immediately.

24. If the dart doesn't launch properly:

i) Launch it by hand and check it flies well.
If not try to make a better one with the other half of the paper.

ii) Make sure you are feeding the paper dart in so that just the body, and not the wings, are gripped by the bottle tops.

iii) Take off the bottle tops and make sure both motors are rotating. It can look as though they are both being driven when one bottle top touches the other one and turns it round. Sometimes the crocodile clips come off due to the vibrations.

iv) Put the bottle tops back on. If there is too big a gap between the bottle tops you can fit more strips of inner tube over the bottle tops.

v) If the gap is much too big (so that it doesn't grip the paper dart) or too small (so that the paper dart jams) you can try thicker or thinner paper for the paper dart. If that doesn't work you could re-drill the holes in the base.

Electrical energy in the circuit is converted to kinetic (movement) energy in the rotating bottle tops. When these grip the paper dart some of this energy is transferred to kinetic energy in the dart. Because the dart is very light it doesn't need much energy to make it travel quite fast.